*A po*

**LOSING A SON TO SUICIDE**
**A POETIC JOURNEY THROUGH GRIEF**

Copyright © 2014 by Randall Stepp. All rights reserved worldwide. No part of this publication may be replicated, redistributed, or given away in any form without the prior written consent of the author/publisher

LOSING A SON TO SUICIDE

This book is dedicated to the memory of
my son and best friend,

Brandon Tyler Stepp.

*"Suicide is comprised of seven letters,
whose sum is greater than the parts.
Within its' narrow confines
lies the wreckage of countless hearts."*

*Excerpt from the poem, "Why?"*

*A poetic journey through grief*

## ABOUT THE AUTHOR

My name is Randall Stepp, and if my life had continued along the path which I had envisioned, you would not be reading these words today. I am a production print technician by trade and now an amateur writer by circumstance. I had never written poetry until suffering the loss of my son and only child Brandon. I have heard people say that everyone has a hidden gift and I guess in my case it took the pain of suicide loss for it to surface. How I wish that I could have lived out my entire life never knowing that I had the uncanny ability to rhyme misery with pain. At the time of this writing I am 44 years old. I remember before losing Brandon, I felt as if my life was reaching its midpoint and time was getting short. But since losing him, I feel as if we are separated by far too many years. I married my high school sweetheart Sherri in August of 1988 and we are still happily married today. I know for some couples, tragedy will often divide them. But in our case it has brought us closer together, I think that it's because I know she understands the pain I live with every day. We lost our son Brandon on October 14, 2010.

LOSING A SON TO SUICIDE

Life before that date now seems like an all too perfect dream that abruptly came to an end on that terrible date. Out of the hurt and despair that followed, this collection of poetry emerged.

*A poetic journey through grief*

# Table of Contents

| | |
|---|---|
| **INTRODUCTION** | 9 |
| **MY STORY** | 11 |
| **IF** | 20 |
| **STEREOTYPE** | 23 |
| **SUICIDE SHATTERS** | 24 |
| **UNSPOKEN JUDGMENTS** | 25 |
| **MY SON** | 26 |
| **SECRET** | 27 |
| **STIGMA** | 28 |
| **SILENT KILLER** | 30 |
| **DEFENDING A MEMORY** | 31 |
| **SUICIDE** | 32 |
| **OCTOBER** | 33 |
| **LEFT BEHIND** | 34 |
| **WHY?** | 36 |
| **WORST FEAR** | 37 |
| **WAVES OF SORROW** | 38 |
| **YOUR CHOICE** | 40 |
| **15** | 44 |
| **LOST** | 45 |
| **DREAMING OF THE DAY** | 46 |
| **MEMORY** | 47 |

- **LEGACY** ............................................. 48
- **QUESTIONS** ...................................... 49
- **GONE** ................................................. 50
- **SEEKING REFUGE** ........................... 51
- **TALK WITH GOD** ............................. 52
- **INSPIRATION** ................................... 54
- **NOW** ................................................... 55
- **NAME** ................................................. 56
- **INTERNAL STRUGGLE** .................... 57
- **GRIEF** ................................................. 58
- **CROSS OVER** .................................... 59
- **LITTLE ANGEL** ................................. 61
- **SURVIVE** ........................................... 62
- **FIRST THANKSGIVING** ................... 63
- **LONGING** .......................................... 64
- **THURSDAY** ....................................... 65
- **WINGS** ............................................... 66
- **LIFE** .................................................... 67
- **ETERNITY** ......................................... 69
- **HELL** ................................................... 70
- **FLASHBACK** ...................................... 71
- **HEAVEN** ............................................ 72
- **YOUR BIRTHDAY** ............................. 73

*A poetic journey through grief*

| | |
|---|---|
| **WHY ME?** | 74 |
| **PRAYER** | 76 |
| **CAUGHT** | 77 |
| **ONE DAY AT A TIME** | 78 |
| **JUST BEYOND** | 79 |
| **PAIN** | 80 |
| **BELIEF** | 81 |
| **MISSING YOU** | 82 |
| **FATHER** | 83 |
| **NEW NORMAL** | 84 |
| **FAILURE** | 86 |
| **NIGHTMARE** | 87 |
| **RETURN** | 88 |
| **VOICE** | 90 |
| **I KNOW** | 92 |
| **HOLE** | 93 |
| **PITY** | 94 |
| **POSITIVE ATTITUDE** | 96 |
| **SON** | 98 |
| **GETAWAY** | 99 |
| **ONE SOUND** | 100 |
| **HE WALKS WITH ME** | 102 |
| **MY FATE** | 104 |

| | |
|---|---|
| **7:30** | 106 |
| **S.O.S** | 107 |
| **SUPPORT GROUP** | 108 |
| **GATHER** | 109 |
| **THIS WALK** | 110 |
| **OUT OF THE DARKNESS** | 112 |
| **SURVIVORS DAY** | 113 |
| **FINAL THOUGHTS** | 114 |

# INTRODUCTION

If you are reading this book, then it is probably because a previously unimaginable event has occurred in your life. And you now know the unique pain and anguish that come with losing a loved one to suicide. It is a grief so deep and so dark that once you have experienced it, you will never be the same person again. You'll discover that grief doesn't present itself in the neat orderly stages which we have all heard of. Instead you may find that you are feeling a multitude of different emotions, all at the same time. In my case, I have discovered that putting my thoughts down on paper helps me to temporarily calm this storm of emotions. Some people write letters, but I always do my writing in the form of poetry. I started writing my first poems within days of my sons' suicide and now several years into my journey, I have written countless poems. I will often read my poetry at the survivors of suicide meetings which I attend, and usually someone will share with me how they have felt the very same way. But whenever someone that hasn't suffered a suicide loss will hear them, they typically don't have much to say. The purpose in sharing my poetry is to let those of you that are newly bereaved know that you are not alone, and what you are feeling is completely normal. If my book can help to comfort just one grieving soul, then my son's death will not have been in vain.

*My family before losing Brandon.*

*A poetic journey through grief*

## MY STORY

Brandon was born on February 23, 1995 and passed away on October 14, 2010. In those brief 15 years of life, he filled each and every day with joy. As our only child he was the center of attention and universe for me and my wife Sherri. Every day would begin with me telling him that I loved him and would end with a goodnight kiss on the head. Now he is gone and my life will never again be the same. He was known to the world as Brandon, but in our home was affectionately called peep. A nickname he acquired as a baby by always peeping to make sure someone was holding him. When he would have friends over to visit, we were always under strict orders to call him Brandon. At 15 you don't want information like that to become known. He shared in my sense of humor and we enjoyed many priceless hours together laughing and joking. Brandon was simply a fun person to be around and I find myself not only mourning the loss of my son, but also my best friend. We enjoyed lifting weights together and spent quite a few evenings at the gym. During our workouts, we would talk about everything. During our conversations I would always attempt to share with him the lessons of life, which I had learned the hard way. Our close relationship just makes his suicide even more difficult to understand. I always thought he would confide in me, if he was ever in trouble. Reconciling his suicide, with the son I knew and loved is something that I fear I may never be able to fully achieve. Brandon was a smart, handsome and talented boy that excelled at almost everything he did. He maintained straight A's in school despite taking honors classes, he was also on the wrestling team and involved in several clubs. But Brandon's greatest love and talent was music, it seemed to flow through him effortlessly. His favorite instrument was the guitar, on which he played everything from heavy metal to classical. The world will never know what all Brandon could have accomplished in his life, given all the talents he possessed. His life's dream was to attend the Air Force Academy and become a pilot. But instead of watching all those dreams become reality, I am left to question why he never turned to me in his final hour.

This is the best account that I can provide concerning the events that led to the loss of my precious son on that terrible October day. That day started out just like any other Thursday, I told

*A poetic journey through grief*

Brandon that I loved him through a closed bathroom door as I was leaving for work. That day the weather was sunny and pleasant for the middle of October. My time at work was so typical that it would have vanished into obscurity had it not been for what transpired upon arriving home that day. If I could have only known of the tragedy that awaited me that evening. I was sitting on the couch when Brandon arrived home from wrestling practice, Sherri and I could instantly sense that something was wrong by the scared look on his face. We repeatedly asked him what was wrong, but he just kept saying that he didn't feel well. I felt of his forehead to see if he had a fever and Sherri rubbed his stomach because he said it hurt. After a few minutes he said he was going upstairs. While we were discussing which restaurant to go to, Brandon must have been getting the .22 rifle that I received as a Christmas gift at the age of twelve, down out of the closet and the ammunition from my dresser. Unknown to us at the time, was the fact that Brandon had sent some texts to his former girlfriend threatening to harm himself. The texts were not recent but the former girlfriend had saved them. And after learning of Brandon having a new girlfriend, she texted him on his way home and informed him that she and her mother were coming to our house to show us the saved texts. That explained why he looked so scared, he must have envisioned us seeing his threats and thinking we would no longer look at him in the same way. Nothing could have been further from the truth though. Once we decided where we were going out to eat at, we called for Brandon and he came downstairs to go with us. He must have thought that once he escaped the situation he could tell us what was going on in his own time. As we were walking towards the front door to leave, the doorbell rang. As Sherri was answering the door, Brandon casually turned and ran upstairs. I just assumed that he had forgotten his phone. After seeing who was at the door, I instinctively ran after him. I guess I could just sense that something was terribly wrong. As I was reaching for the door to Brandon's guitar room, I heard the sound that will haunt me for the rest of my life. As I opened the door, time seemed to stop and I watched in horror as my entire world came crashing down. I was so close to stopping this nightmare, that I actually saw my boy as he was falling. It was as if I was watching myself in some tragic movie, I could hear myself pleading with Brandon to wake up and telling him how much I loved him. But Brandon never regained consciousness and I only pray that he heard me telling him how much he was loved and knew that he was not alone. We officially lost him about two hours later after he was air lifted to the University Medical Center in Louisville. That drive home from the hospital was the most surreal experience of my life, how can you have a child at five o'clock and lose them forever by seven. And how could he have been so scared and not come to me and tell me what was going on. To know your child was that panicked and worried in their last moments of life is something that I will never be able to get over or put behind me. I was right there and yet he must have felt as if he were all alone in the world. If I could have only gotten there in time to knock the gun away, then he would have had the chance to realize all that he was throwing away. But instead, I am left behind to struggle with these questions, for which there will never be any answers. I always knew that I loved Brandon with all my heart, but until you lose a child, it is impossible to fully realize how woven they are into the very fabric of your soul. Without them, dreams of the future disappear and all worries about your own mortality are gone as well. You will now view your life through the prism of suicide, dividing it into two parts. The first part is gone forever and what you are left with is something referred to as the new normal. I first heard that term at a survivors of suicide meeting, I attended a mere week after losing Brandon. I remember the feeling of relief that came with being amongst a group of people that could relate to what I was feeling, because they had all been there. If you have been hesitant to share your story with others, I would highly recommend that you find a support group in your area. It was my local group that got me through that terrible first year, and now several years later I still attend, though now it is mainly to help those that are newly bereaved. Once you meet a fellow survivor of suicide, you will discover that there is an instant connection. Because we are all now members of a club, which none of us ever requested to join. We all wear the scarlet letter of suicide, which brings with it a feeling that was unknown to me before losing Brandon. That feeling is the stigma of suicide, which in the beginning is overwhelming. You will find yourself avoiding certain social situations or individuals because you suddenly feel like an outcast of society. But if you will freely share your story, you will find that others will open up about their experiences with suicide. Truth is the only weapon we have in this fight against the secrecy and shame of suicide. This book is my contribution to that battle, hopefully it will provide you a small amount of reassurance that you are not alone on your journey.

On the proceeding pages you will find my collection of poetry, and my thoughts on certain selections. If you are a poetry critic looking for proper form and composition then I am truly sorry. All I have to offer you is honesty and raw emotion. I hope that my poems will resonate with you, and provide you a small bit of comfort. If you haven't suffered such a loss, they will offer you a glimpse into the carnage left behind when you lose someone you love to suicide. I wrote the majority of my poetry during that terrible first year, when just making it to the next moment seemed almost impossible. Now nearly four years later, many of them seem as if they were written by a stranger. You will find that much of the whole first year will seem surreal, because you are still in shock and denial a majority of the time. If I could only give you one word of advice to help you with your grief, it would be to forget the word should. Don't worry about what you should do, instead do what you can do. Grieving is hard enough without the added burden of living up to someone else's expectations of what you should or shouldn't be doing. So just be true to yourself and listen to your heart as you start down this long difficult road.

Brandon's beautiful smile.

*A poetic journey through grief*

One of the first poems I wrote is simply entitled "If". It was written in the first few weeks after losing Brandon. I remember repeatedly replaying the events surrounding that day and his suicide. I would imagine all the things that I would have done differently if only I had known. I think some part of me actually believed that if I could dream up an alternate scenario, then somehow Brandon would return to me. I can say from experience that with time the compulsive need to retell your story will become less and less intense. But until then, you just have to keep sharing your story until you no longer have the urge to do so. The time required for this to happen will be different for every individual. Just be kind to yourself and grieve at your own pace, and remember that you are writing your own story as you go.

## If

If I had known that you were hurting
when you came home that day.
I would've wrapped my arms around you
and told you it's okay.

You don't have to be ashamed
of having a broken heart.
Life is full of ups and downs
and this is just a part.

I love you more
than you could ever understand.
And I'm always here for you
when you need a helping hand.

It doesn't matter to me
what you have said or done.
Into the safety of my arms
you can always run.

I know that you're not perfect
and mistakes you'll surely make.
When I see you hurting
it causes my heart to break.

So just know that I love you
and I always will.
And you might not believe it
but I know how you feel.

Then I would kiss you on the head
and hug you so tight
You would be smiling
knowing everything's alright.

If I could turn back time
that is what I would say.
But I did not know
on that terrible day.

Writing that poem didn't rewrite history or magically bring Brandon back, but it did help to get me through the next few days after I wrote it. And in the beginning of your grief, simply making it to the next minute is a major accomplishment. So if you are able to do so, I highly recommend that you put your feelings down on paper in some form. Some find it helpful to write letters to their loved ones, while others simply organize lists of all the things that they wished they would have said or done. And if you don't feel comfortable sharing, then shred or burn them when you are done. Just getting the thoughts out of your head will provide you at least some temporary relief.

LOSING A SON TO SUICIDE

The next several poems are all focused on the stigma of suicide. It is my attempt to express how our loved ones were so much more than their final decision. When you tell outsiders that your child completed suicide, normally you will get that distant stare of judgment. That look that implies your child must have been unhappy, troubled or defective in some way. But I refuse to let Brandon's suicide redefine the fifteen precious years I shared with him. Suicide may have claimed my son's life, but it will never do the same to his memory. To help me in my writing, I often envision suicide as a silent predator. For some it kills quickly, others it may stalk for years before finally going in for the kill. And even though most believe that suicide could never touch their lives, I think that under the right set of circumstances anyone could succumb to this cold and indiscriminate killer.

*A poetic journey through grief*

# STEREOTYPE

Some will stereotype the victim
when it comes to suicide.
You'll never know my loved one
peering in from the outside.

You never heard their laughter
or saw the beauty of their smile.
If you think that you're above this
then your living in denial.

It can happen in an instant
as chance and circumstance collide.
Left to grieve a son or daughter
while others judge the way they died.

No family is ever immune
to this heartache or this pain.
I once stood beside you in the sunshine
as others struggled through the rain.

So when you hear me tell my story
please offer more than a distant stare.
The fate which I now suffer
could be one we someday share.

## Suicide Shatters

Suicide is a parasite.
feeds off secrecy and shame.
Whispers ever so quietly
that you're the one to blame.

This could have been prevented.
why didn't you just open up your eyes?
Delights in your suffering
as it tells you all its lies.

How can you go on living?
it implies with a stare.
You're supposed to suffer
to show how much you care.

Regrets overwhelm you.
the guilt too much to bear.
It has you where it wants you
and determined to keep you there.

The only way to stop it's taunting
is to call it by its name
Drag it out of the darkness
ending its cruel game.

*A poetic journey through grief*

# UNSPOKEN JUDGMENTS

Suicide so evil,
so dark and so cold.
All the infinite questions
one action can hold.

Creates hell on earth
for those left behind.
Compassion from others
fades quickly, you'll find.

No rest for the weary
the world just goes on.
Like they don't even notice
your loved one is gone.

All the unspoken judgments
you hear in your mind.
Either real or imagined
can be so unkind.

You've lost your whole world
no one speaks their name.
Is it ignorance and fear
or stigma and shame.

But I won't be silent
to blend into the crowd.
My son did exist
and I'll forever be proud.

## My Son

My son was more
than some sad story.
Or a cruel life lesson
to show God's glory.

He was my whole life,
my source of joy.
Such a beautiful soul
He was my boy.

Don't judge his life
by a single mistake.
Which in the wrong situation,
anyone could make.

Keep his spirit with us,
don't let suicide erase.
All the priceless memories
of his smiling face.

So, please say his name often
he was a person kind and true.
Tragedy is not selective,
next time it could be you.

*A poetic journey through grief*

# SECRET

As the shock begins to fade
from losing my son so dear.
I'm still broken on the inside
but I've cried out every tear.

Everyone else has moved on
my loss is yesterday's news.
They would be more sympathetic
if forced to walk in my shoes.

But their world remains unchanged
they can't imagine my pain.
Leaving me feeling like an outsider
in a place, I'm forced to remain.

Two opposing realities
that I live in everyday.
I would love to be myself
not this role, I have to play.

Although it seems I've returned
to the person you once knew.
Underneath this normal exterior
lies the truth, I share with few.

A broken and homesick spirit
with a secret I keep inside.
Forced to remain among the living
after a part of me has died.

## STIGMA

Suicide has such a stigma
attached to its name.
It takes once proud parents
and paints them with shame.

In the causes for a death
it's a reason rarely spoken.
It should be viewed as dying
from a spirit that's broken.

In one moment of weakness
they made a terrible choice.
They are not here to express it
so, I am giving them a voice.

By this one act
we cannot be defined.
We were so much more
to those we left behind.

We were the precious children
you taught how to walk.
The very best of friends
with whom you could talk.

We loved and we laughed
we brightened up your day.
We completed your world
in our own special way.

We'll forever be remembered
for our final mistake.
And we are so sorry
for the hearts we did break.

So when you hear of a suicide
look beyond the ugly word.
There you will find a person
with a story to be heard.

## Silent killer

Suicide so elusive
lies hidden in plain sight.
Can stalk its prey for decades.
or devour you in a night

It begins as a whisper
grows louder day by day.
It sells itself as an option
while omitting the price you pay.

Meditations on the consequences
are distracted by its screams.
Feeding off human misery
thriving on broken dreams.

It seduces you with the drama
picturing reactions in your mind.
Numbs you to the impact
on those you leave behind.

Deadly thoughts and circumstance
combine with deadly force.
A future of hope and happiness
has taken a different course.

A precious life has ended
through deception and deceit.
Another family has fallen victim
suicides mission is complete.

*A poetic journey through grief*

# DEFENDING A MEMORY

I'm a suicide survivor
broken and slow to mend.
All that remains is a memory
which I'm left here to defend.

People are so judgmental
always so quick to decide.
My son was so much more
than the way in which he died.

When someone hears of a suicide
they picture a poor tortured soul.
Not a kind and gentle kid
in a situation gone out of control.

A dreadful chain of events
placed his back to the wall.
One terrible choice later
I have forever lost it all.

I just want people to know
the boy that was my best friend.
He was not just another statistic
that met with a tragic end.

All I have left is his story
which I will continue to tell.
In the hopes others will listen
and come to know him as well.

# SUICIDE

Suicide is such a terrible word
full of hurt and pain.
It takes years of precious memories
and marks them with a stain.

Missing my son so badly
and constantly wondering why.
I know to the core of my being
he did not want to die.

It was just an impulsive reaction
brought on by fear.
That has broken all the hearts
that held him so dear.

One fatal mistake
for which there is no relief.
All I'm left with are memories
and never ending grief.

But you can't hug a memory
or hold it close and tight.
Suicide claimed two more lives
on that October night.

*A poetic journey through grief*

# OCTOBER

In the beginning of October
all the world was right.
For the blessings of our home
I thanked God every night.

Our family was happy
everything was in its' place.
Always joking with my boy
how I loved his smiling face.

In the middle of October
all was destroyed from inside.
It seems from out of nowhere
my son committed suicide.

Going through the checklist
he showed not a single sign.
I will never understand
what was going through his mind.

At the end of October
disbelief and shock remain.
I never thought it possible
for a heart to hold such pain.

Dreams of the future
have all faded to black.
This life is so unfair
I want my boy back.

My life has been altered
and gone so far off course.
Cursed to live on a diet
of guilt and remorse.

# Left Behind

Whenever a suicide is committed
a dream is laid to rest.
Mourned by the people
that loved and knew them best.

All the aspirations
and promise they once held.
Now all lie buried
and you feel as if you've failed.

In their darkest hour
you were nowhere to be found.
All the guilt and second guessing,
regrets abound.

Every word left unsaid
haunts you in the night.
But you can never go back
to make things right.

If you only had the chance
to say one last goodbye.
But you were denied that
and are left to wonder why.

Forced to repeat your questions
until you no longer care.
Why they had to leave you
or why it's so unfair.

*A poetic journey through grief*

You just want them back
to hold in a long embrace.
Let them know you love them
and see their precious face.

But the only satisfaction
a survivor will ever find.
Is known in preventing
another tragedy of this kind.

# WHY?

Suicide is comprised of seven letters
whose sum is greater than the parts.
Within its' narrow confines
lies the wreckage of countless hearts.

A lifetime full of questions
contained in a single word.
You could repeat them forever
but the answers remain unheard.

Each day brings a new puzzle
you only lack the final piece.
How do you come to accept
that the questions will never cease.

The only person with the answers
is now a lifetime away.
Leaving you to keep asking
why they left you in this way.

No matter how you try
you can never stop your quest.
In your fruitless search for answers
you won't find a moments rest.

The end to your chronic affliction
will come on the day that you die.
And not until your very last breath
Will you utter your final…why?

*A poetic journey through grief*

# WORST FEAR

Every parents' nightmare
is the reality I face.
The life that I once knew
is gone without a trace.

My son I loved so dearly
is missing from my sight.
My world forever changed
in the course of just one night.

What most could not imagine
I have now lived through.
I lost my heart, I lost my soul
and all I thought was true.

My eyes forever wounded
by a sight no one should see.
Witnessing as your future
becomes a memory.

Now, I stand here empty
an orphaned parent in disbelief.
Living a life I never planned on,
expectations replaced by grief.

## WAVES OF SORROW

Suicide is like a boat
speeding across a calm lake.
Leaving turmoil and destruction
behind in its wake.

The boat quickly disappears
unaware of its toll.
Its' waves break the spirit
and devastate the soul.

The water is crowded with people
that loved the boater so.
Why he would ever do such a thing
they will never know.

Didn't he realize the damage
this tide would impose.
All the innocent victims
to this hell he'd expose.

Lives are rocked and capsized
by the swells that are made.
Why into such a serene lake
would this vessel invade.

The closer you were to the boat
the greater your cost.
Figured by totaling
hopes and dreams you've lost.
.

*A poetic journey through grief*

But you can't question his motives
for he is now gone.
Only the chaos he's caused
is left to live on.

He has now departed
and is immune to the pain.
You are left to struggle
in the waves that remain.

If somehow you endure
and make it back to the shore.
You will be left broken
and haunted evermore.

## YOUR CHOICE

I have loved you completely
since the day you were born.
Never did I imagine
I would be left here to mourn.

No father should know the pain
of having a son laid to rest.
I can still picture you sleeping
that first night on my chest.

I don't think I even slept
I was so afraid you would fall.
Now by your own hand
I have forever lost it all.

I tried so hard to protect you
from all the worlds sins.
But death didn't come from the outside
it came from within.

How could you choose
to shade me from your light.
To commit such a wrong
that can never be made right.

You never disappointed me
in the course of your life.
Only in your departing
did you bring me any strife.

Now I'm left to suffer
and forever wonder why.
I will never understand
no matter how hard I try.

*A poetic journey through grief*

The son that I knew
filled my heart with pride.
He was not the type
to ever think of suicide.

Suicide is the dominion
of the desperate and alone.
He had a loving family
and warm and peaceful home.

Suicide was like an intruder
that wandered in one day.
Took everything I valued
and silently crept away.

All I have left are longings
that will never be fulfilled.
No one can ever revive
all this suicide has killed.

The next poem entitled "15", is the age Brandon will forever stay. It was my way of coming to terms with the new reality I was faced with after Brandon's suicide. It is still one of the most difficult ones for me to read, because it summarizes all of the milestones in Brandon's life that will never become a reality. As mine and Sherri's only child he held all of our hopes and dreams for the future. And now we are forced to come to the sad realization that we will never see Brandon get married or have children. It is this loss of expectations that makes any death difficult to deal with, but when you add the baggage of suicide to the equation. It can sometimes be overwhelming and leave you feeling cheated by life. I sometimes have to fight the urge to just call myself a victim and give up, but I know that Brandon's memory deserves more of a tribute than that. One thing that gets me through the tough times is to visualize that glorious day when me and Brandon are finally reunited. I can just imagine that proud look on his face when he hears of all the acts of kindness that were performed in his memory. I now look at my life as a living tribute to my son. I would urge you to do the same when you are strong

*A poetic journey through grief*

enough to consider such things. If we don't keep our loved ones memory alive by helping others in their name, then they will needlessly suffer a second death. But in the first few years, you just need to focus on your own grief until you have healed enough to see beyond it. Most experts recommend that you wait at least two years before attempting to offer support to others in our situation. It takes at least that long to be able to listen to someone tell their story, without feeling the need to share your own. So just be patient and take care of yourself first. And when the time comes, you will be able to be there for someone else in their time of need.

Following "15", you will find a variety of poems that deal with the heartache and pain of suicide loss. I would have put them in chronological order, but I sadly neglected to date them at the time. And with the shock of suicide, comes the loss of memory. So looking back, I don't recall when I wrote most of them. But the emotions they express are ones you can relate to whether your loss was yesterday or twenty years ago.

## 15

In our hearts and minds
you will never age a day.
Vibrant, young, and full of life
you will always stay.

There will never be a wrinkle
on your lovely face.
Life's many joys and disappointments
never will you taste.

All the new memories
that will always remain unknown.
Never to go to college
or move out on your own.

No beautiful bride
for you to raise the veil and kiss.
And your own child's laughter
is a sound that you will miss.

No watching Mom and Dad
as they slowly grow old.
All the jokes and funny stories
that never will be told.

All you could have done
to make this world a better place.
Has vanished from existence
with the absence of your face

How could the hands of fate
be so cruel and cold.
That our son will forever be
fifteen years old.

*A poetic journey through grief*

# LOST

I have lost my way
in this labyrinth of grief.
I have no hope of escaping
and unable to get relief.

Time passes by without me.
I can't stop it, though I've tried.
still can't accept the reality
That part of me has died.

I tell myself you'll be back soon
anything to avoid the pain.
But I grow so tired of waiting.
for the sun, amidst this rain.

Just an empty shell
of the man I was before.
Suicide takes everything
keeps coming back for more.

Trapped in a nightmare
left stranded without my son.
All my dreams of the future
have been reduced to none.

# Dreaming of the Day

I curse the sun for rising
without your face to shine upon.
Damn the world for turning
how can it, when you're gone.

It only hurts with every heartbeat
living without you here.
Your memory seems more distant
with every month and every year.

How I long to hold you
see your blue eyes once again.
I was so proud to be your father
so lucky to call you friend.

I often dream of eternity
when the broken will be whole.
Until again I see you
you will live on in my soul.

## MEMORY

I don't want you as a memory
I just want you as my son.
To dream of all you will do
not reminisce about what you've done.

To again live in the present
not consumed by the past.
Fifteen years of memories
will never be enough to last.

You left me in midsentence
without a chance to say goodbye.
With a lifetime full of images
that will haunt me until I die.

Time proceeds without me
trapped in a suspended state.
Held captive by the calendar
and its' October 14th date.

That day marks the birth
of the person I am today.
The closing of your blue eyes
has left my world forever gray.

## LEGACY

I survived the death of me
and now live to tell the tale.
As you were on your way to heaven
you dropped me off in hell.

I know you never meant this
but I'm left to pay the toll.
A chorus of a thousand questions
echoes through my soul.

Yet somehow I keep on going
surviving without you here.
Gathering strength from your memory
I grow stronger year by year.

In my mind I can hear you
urging me to live again.
To forge a lasting legacy
not dwell, on what could have been.

Reality is a cruel master
in whose domain I must exist.
I pray in time, God will heal my heart
help me to lower my angry fist.

The time that separates us
is a void that I must fill.
With bitterness and resentment
or kindness and goodwill.

When I finally make it to you
I hope that I can say.
Your life inspired, love and kindness
not self-destruction and dismay.

*A poetic journey through grief*

# QUESTIONS

I wake up in the morning
and they find me at first light.
All these questions that I carry
welcome to my plight.

I'm a suicide survivor
living a life I never chose.
The questions are relentless
but the answers, no one knows.

All the whys and what ifs
Always running through my head.
Second guessing almost everything
that was ever done or said.

How could he leave me?
without a chance to say goodbye.
Why didn't I see it coming?
they'll never be an answer why.

Waiting until this life's over
for this torture to finally end.
Time may heal some wounds.
but others it can never mend.

## GONE

As I sit alone in silence
my heart cries out your name.
This primal need to hold you
that death will never tame.

Time keeps on moving forward
leaving me stranded far behind.
Lost and searching for the answers
that aren't there for me to find.

The years divide us like a chasm
that grows wider day by day.
God ignores my pleas to bridge it
indifferent to my dismay.

My thoughts forever raging
hard to focus on just one.
A single theme that keeps repeating
is I can't believe you're gone.

*A poetic journey through grief*

## SEEKING REFUGE

Angry at the sunrise
for revealing you're not here.
What seems a nightmare in the darkness
the dawn makes all too clear.

Days and months without you
are turning into years.
I've surrendered to the sadness
tired of fighting back the tears.

Overwhelmed by depression
my existence seems in vain.
As pointless as my poetry
rhyming misery with pain.

Sleep is my only refuge
dreaming of what could have been.
Until I wake up to reality
and lose you once again.

# TALK WITH GOD

From one father to another
that has lost an only son.
I am caught in this storm
and have nowhere left to run.

I just feel so hopeless
and I can't face another day.
God, I come to you broken
and on my knees I pray.

Please pour out your love
and heal this broken heart.
My whole world's been shattered
and everything is torn apart.

I am at your mercy God
please answer me in some way.
And after searching my heart
I think this is what God would say.

Run into my arms child
because I know just how you feel.
Although, you do not understand
someday, I will reveal.

The reason for this lesson
which now seems so unkind.
There is a hidden gift
that you will one day find.

*A poetic journey through grief*

Perhaps a life in my service
which you never would've known.
Sometimes tears are needed
to nourish the seeds I've sown.

I too have lost a son
that was the apple of my eye.
Jesus had to suffer
so your dear son will never die.

The shackles of the grave
have been broken by his grace.
So that you can once again
see your son's lovely face.

It is just a temporary separation
that will in eternity seem so brief.
I am so glad to finally hear from you
I'm sorry it took this grief.

I open up my arms
and happily welcome you home.
Remember, I am always by your side
you will never walk alone

# INSPIRATION

I want to honor your memory
help the hurting in your name.
That's what I keep saying
as I'm mired in all this pain.

I have so many good intentions
without the will to see them through.
You were such an inspiration
it's the least that I could do.

Leave a legacy in your honor
comfort the broken and alone.
I need your love to guide me
I can't do this on my own.

Help me have compassion
for others who share my plight.
Let me see beyond myself
and do what I know is right.

I dream of the day I'll join you
I can just imagine what you'll say.
I'm so glad that I inspired you
to help others along the way.

*A poetic journey through grief*

# Now

I yearn to hear your voice,
afraid I'll forget the sound.
Scared to watch home movies
they hurt too much, I've found.

Even though you're gone
I still speak to you each day.
Sounds like I've gone insane
since you've gone away.

All your baby pictures
are just too hard to see.
Like some tragic movie,
knowing what the end will be.

I can't go into your bedroom
untouched since that day.
A shrine to what used to be
too painful a price to pay.

Just looking in the doorway
Brings on dread and fear.
I have become another person
now that you're not here.

## Name

Whenever someone dies
we lose a precious soul.
For loved ones left behind
the silence takes its toll.

Please speak of them often
free their memory to roam.
Every time that they are mentioned
a part of them comes home.

Share the special moments
that made you love them so.
What seems a simple gesture
means more than you could know.

Don't avoid their name
remembering helps to ease the pain.
You'll never know the value
to all the loved ones that remain.

Just sharing a single story
can brighten up a day.
Reassures a grieving soul
that memories never pass away

*A poetic journey through grief*

# INTERNAL STRUGGLE

Badly bruised and broken
yet somehow here I stand.
Everything I held so tightly
has slipped right through my hand.

Left without a purpose
or a plan to guide my way.
I can't find you in tomorrow
so I cling to yesterday.

My head and heart conspire
to give me solace, amidst my grief.
Deluding me from reality
living in denial and disbelief.

Passing the time with distractions
diversions to get through the day.
Hoping the truth never finds me
growing weary of running away.

In my mind a battle is raging
happy memories and horrific scenes.
Momentum is constantly shifting
living in limbo in between.

No matter the ultimate victor
no prize is left to be won.
Memories may console for a moment
but can't change the fact that you're
gone.

# GRIEF

Wandering through this lifetime,
searching for a purpose in my pain.
Is there a point to all this suffering
or is it all in vain?

Dreams of you returning
have slowly died away.
Reality takes hold now
I must accept you've passed away.

With every waking second
my heart screams out your name.
Longing for what used to be,
wanting things to be the same.

Vanished like a vapor,
the life that I once knew.
Seems too terrible to fathom,
none of this seems true.

Empathy and compassion
disappear as time goes by.
Left to grieve the child I loved
and never know the reason why.

The years disperse the crowd
that once offered me relief.
Grief may endure forever
but peoples sympathy is brief.

*A poetic journey through grief*

# CROSS OVER

One foot in heaven
the other still here.
How I long to cross over
and shed my last tear.

My mind starts to ponder
what heaven will be.
Is it someplace familiar,
are you waiting for me?

Am I already with you
on an alternate plane.
Making up for this sadness
no hint of this pain.

Am I even aware
I suffered this fate.
Did I get there in time
and not a moment too late.

Do I get to watch
as you live out your dreams.
That would be justice
At least it seems.

Every missed milestone
would be cherished much more.
Maybe it takes time in hell
to know what heaven is for.

The following poem requires a little bit of explanation. When Brandon was still very young, he asked us on a few different occasions if we remembered when he was a bird. At the time we just laughed and told him that he was never a bird. But after losing him I began to wonder, what if he could have remembered a time before coming to this earth. I envisioned him as a beautiful angel that was simply returning home.

*A poetic journey through grief*

# LITTLE ANGEL

When you were still a toddler
around the age of three.
You could still remember
the angel you used to be.

You said on a few occasions
"remember when I was a bird".
Although we didn't know it then
of your time in Heaven, we heard.

You could still recall
when God knew you before.
Now you have departed
and soar with wings once more.

Mommy's little angel
we called you with such love.
Now you're one of heaven's angels
smiling down from above.

When again we see you
our eyes will fill with tears.
For we have missed our little angel
through all these lonely years.

# Survive

I make it through another hour,
and then a day, a week, a year.
The time all blurs together
an endless stream of hurt and fear.

My life has been molested
touched by suicide's dark hand.
It has stolen my identity
and the future I had planned.

I'm in a struggle for survival
a daily battle to make it through.
The only thing that keeps me going
is the love I have for you.

To leave a lasting legacy
so your passing was not in vain.
Rise like a phoenix from the ashes
find my purpose amidst this pain.


I will help others in your memory
so that when all is said and done.
The world will be left a little kinder
because a father loved his son.

*A poetic journey through grief*

# FIRST THANKSGIVING

The first Thanksgiving day
since the loss of my son.
Reasons to be thankful
I have almost none.

I'm thankful for the memories
and years we got to spend.
But I'm angry with your choice
and its' suicidal end.

I'm thankful for the chance
to love with all my heart.
But I'm so hurt by your decision
it tore my world apart.

I'm thankful God blessed me
with a son as kind as you.
But I'm confused by your action
it doesn't fit the boy I knew.

I'm thankful that I'll see you
on the other side of death.
But the heartache's so consuming
it hurts with every breath.

So on this first Thanksgiving
I'll just survive the day.
Now that all my blessing's
have suddenly gone away.

# Longing

How few are the tears of a lifetime
when compared to eternal joy.
This suffering will be but a memory
of a season without my boy.

A window of time in the darkness
to make me yearn for the light.
I know that happiness awaits me
at the end of this cold, dark night.

As brief as the space between heartbeats
will be our time lived apart.
I don't understand God's reasons
but I will continue to trust His heart.

He has promised a new day is coming
where death will no longer divide.
Heaven is a place of reunions
where brokenness cannot abide.

So I fix my eyes on eternity
I know that my longing ends there.
My sorrows will be forgotten
along with the hurt and despair.

# THURSDAY

It was just an ordinary Thursday
when my world came to an end.
That day I lost my future,
my son and my best friend.

The ringing of the doorbell
served as the starting gun.
In a race against fate
no man should have to run.

I finished one step behind
all my hopes and dreams.
I watched as they unraveled
and fell apart at the seams.

My story had been rewritten
all my plans were made in vain.
My life so full of happiness
was now replaced with pain.

Now an ordinary Thursday
is something I'll never know again.
Now they're just weekly reminders
of the life that could've been.

## WINGS

On my knees in prayer
in the presence of the King.
Pleading for a vision
of what this suffering will bring.

A glimpse into the future
when every tear is wiped away.
A fleeting taste of Heaven
to keep me until that day.

Give me the wings of an eagle
to soar above this pain.
See things from your perspective
and know my loss is not in vain.

Lord of all creation
speak peace into my soul.
Reassure my doubting mind
that someday I'll be whole.

Convince me I can make it
through life without my son.
Sustain me with your presence
to allow me to go on.

Hide me from the heartache
that finds me every day.
Reveal to me your glory
to guide me along the way.

Until I cross the river Jordan
and walk upon the shore.
With all the hurt behind me
and remembered nevermore.

# LIFE

What kind of life is it
when you only long for death.
That is my only motivation
for taking my next breath.

No one can live forever
I keep repeating in my head.
At least I'm one day closer
to the day that I am dead.

My only reason for living
is to gain Heaven's reward.
To again be with my son
and in the presence of the Lord.

I pray for that day to get here
because it hurts so bad to wait.
I can just picture my boy
standing by Heaven's gate.

It will be worth all the suffering
when I finally see his face.
And my weary, tortured soul
can leave this painful place.

The following poem "Eternity" is one that confronted a constant fear I had following Brandon's suicide. I was raised to believe that there was a hell and that certain people were destined to go there. And suicides were among those that would spend their eternity there. After many hours of research and soul searching on the subject, my beliefs have changed greatly. But this is not a forum for sharing my religious views, except to say this. God is love and love doesn't punish innocent people for the mistakes that they make. We all know that our loved ones were not perfect, they were merely human and as such made mistakes. But I think we belittle God when we perceive ourselves as more forgiving than Him. Deep within my heart I know that our loved ones are at peace and one day we will be reunited with them. So if this is a subject that is causing you undo worry during this difficult time, I would encourage you to do your own research into the origins of hell and put your mind at ease. Sorry for my preaching, but relieving people of this worry is one thing that I am truly passionate about. Because I know how deeply it troubled me during the first year. If I have offended your religious views then I sincerely apologize, it definitely was not my intention to do so.

# ETERNITY

All suicides go to hell
I have heard people say.
What would make someone speak
or believe in such a way.

We serve a loving God
who has a fathers heart.
He judges our whole life
not just the final part.

He knows of the weakness
of our flesh and bone.
Of the fear and heartache
our loved one's had known.

He sees within us
to the person inside.
With love and compassion
he will then decide.

He loves us so deeply
he sacrificed his son.
I know of that pain
and would suffer it for none.

I am just a man
with his world torn apart.
I forgive my son completely
for breaking my heart.

So it's from this perspective
I know I can say.
We'll reunite with our loved ones
in Heaven someday.

# Hell

Am I still living
or residing in Hell.
Not much of a difference
from what I can tell.

Questions always burning
tormenting my mind.
Its' been over three years now
since you left me behind.

Everything looks familiar
all that's missing is you.
I pray it's a nightmare
but sadly it's true.

To lose someone so special
and be forced to live on.
Maybe Hells my new normal
now that you're gone.

*A poetic journey through grief*

# FLASHBACK

Noise breaks the silence
awakens fear from deep within.
Transported to that dreadful day
reliving it once again.

Damaged spirit, damaged soul
unwanted keepsakes from the past.
Trapped in mid-October
how much longer can it last.

Racing thoughts and vivid memories
mementos I can't lose.
Nerves forever shaken
a fate no one would choose.

All I am is a shadow,
a remnant of flesh and bone.
No matter how many surround me
this battle I face all alone.

Living has turned into surviving
left off balance and always on guard.
Fearing the next disturbance
could destroy a heart so scarred.

# Heaven

When I take my last breath
and leave this world behind.
I have no doubts or fears
about what I'll see or find.

My son will be waiting
with his arms open wide.
I will run through heavens' gate
to get to his side.

The world without his smile
was such a heartless place.
But all is forgiven
with the sight of his face.

I will have so much to say
but I won't speak a word.
I'll hug him so tightly
that all will be heard.

My spirit will soar
as once again we meet.
And at long last
my heart will be complete.

*A poetic journey through grief*

# YOUR BIRTHDAY

Your birthday came without you,
like it will for all my years.
Balloons drift into the distance
as I wipe away the tears.

My thoughts begin to wander
I'm alone among a crowd.
You would have been 18,
and I would have been so proud.

Your memory is another year older,
but you haven't aged a day.
Left to carry on without you,
You're missed more than words can say.

A cause for celebration
has been robbed of all its joy.
I stand here empty handed,
a lonely father without his boy.

# Why Me?

Why me God? is a question
always going through my head.
I try not to indulge in self-pity
so I leave it all unsaid.

Why did I lose my son
that I loved with all my heart.
His life story was not yet written
it was merely at its start.

He was only fifteen
There was so much left undone.
Why didn't you step in
and save my only son.

It all just seems so pointless
please Lord, just tell me why.
From the darkness of my heart
I listen to God's reply.

This you should have asked me
before suffering all this pain.
Why did you enjoy the sunshine
while others endured the rain.

Why did you know such happiness
in your life before.
When tragedy was then visiting
at someone else's door.

Why were you so blessed
with fifteen glorious years.
While others pray for a child
but receive only tears.

Why did I send my only son
to die upon the cross.
So yours will be a temporary
and not a permanent loss.

This life is but a vapor
and again, your son you'll see.
It is for all these reasons
you should say, oh God why me.

# PRAYER

Lord, I come to you humbled
and on my knees in prayer.
You know the loss I've suffered
it's a common bond we share.

You offered your son freely
with mine, I had no say.
Now you've been reunited
while mine's still so far away.

Others have known your presence
in matters that seem so slight.
But I've been excluded from your mercy
and shielded from your light.

I don't ask for worldly things
they offer me no peace.
I only pray for comfort
and for this torment to cease.

But my prayers all go unanswered
it seems, I'm on my own.
Waiting in this darkness
for your spirit to be shown.

I pray one day you'll hear me
because I know you understand.
I'm just an earthly father
in need of a heavenly hand.

*A poetic journey through grief*

# CAUGHT

I'm caught between two worlds
the living and the dead.
One contains my body
the other occupies my head.

I still remain among the living
and deal with earthly strife.
But without my son beside me
there's no meaning in this life.

It seems as if the world
mocks me with their smiles.
Why does God allow some people
to escape these worldly trials.

They look forward to tomorrow
and the hope of a brighter day.
While I'm forever in October
watching my future pass away.

Everyday I long to cross over
and leave this cold world behind.
Only beyond deaths threshold
will I find my peace of mind.

But God will determine my timing
that is not for me to decide.
I just pray he'll show his mercy
and welcome me home to his side.

# One Day at a Time

One day at a time
is a phrase everyone has heard.
But until you're faced with a tragedy
no one understands a word.

If you had to imagine your life
beyond the scope of the day.
Your inherent will to live
would wither and fade away.

Just getting from minute to minute
is a monumental feat.
When thinking of your family
missing who made it complete.

In my case it's my son
who is no longer by my side.
All my hope for a brighter tomorrow
vanished the day that he died.

I continue to live out of habit
in a world so empty and cold.
I don't even stop to consider
what heartache the future will hold.

Maybe God took my son for some purpose
one which I see no reason or rhyme.
So I'll keep praying for God's mercy
and surviving one day at a time.

# JUST BEYOND

Just beyond the doorway
on the other side of death.
You will find paradise
after taking your last breath.

Dearly departed loved ones
are waiting there for you.
To erase all the sorrow
that you've suffered through.

Homesick no longer
your spirit is free.
All you once wished for
you'll finally see.

Forgotten are the questions
you carried for so long.
Your soul is at rest now
you are where you belong.

With the goodbyes behind you
and only reunions ahead.
it resurrects a part of you
that you once thought was dead.

# PAIN

Life is for the living
I've heard some people say.
But to me it's just an obstacle
standing in my way.

I am like an unhappy worker
watching the clock.
Sitting and waiting
not wanting to talk.

Suffering through the minutes
and biding my time.
Until at life's end
some relief I might find.

My son is in paradise
while I'm trapped in hell.
For just one more embrace
my very soul I would sell.

The dull constant heartbreak
too intense to explain.
Why does God make it possible
to feel such a pain.

*A poetic journey through grief*

# BELIEF

Lord can you hear me
when I'm calling.
I've fell so far
and I'm still falling.

I've lost my son
and my tomorrow.
Misplaced my faith
amidst this sorrow.

Behind me now
my old religion.
That believed my loss
was your decision.

I know, you are love
and impart no pain.
So my belief in you
will still remain.

Despite what others
claim you do.
I will cling to your goodness
and pray it is true.

## Missing You

When I'm missing you so badly
and it's more than I can bear.
I escape into my memories
I can always find you there.

I close my eyes and I'm with you
on a bright and sunny day.
Looking at your smiling face
it's like you never went away.

I wrap my arms around you
and hold you in a long embrace.
My weary eyes end their searching
and settle upon your face.

I tell you how much I love you
and how I miss you more each day.
My heart is restored for a moment
until my delusion slowly fades away.

If I could only stay in my daydream
that's where I'd choose to remain.
There in the warmth of your presence
I find shelter from all this pain.

# FATHER

Every boy needs a father
I would often tell my son.
They've always got your back
no matter what you've done.

All of life's little lessons
I tried so hard to impart.
Did you just forget them
or ignore me from the start.

He knew I'd always be there
with a caring heart and open arms.
I'd never fail to protect him
from this world and all its harms.

But I was denied the chance
to prove how much I cared.
How could he not turn to me
after all the times we shared.

Now I'm staring at a future
devoid of hope and joy.
Never could I have imagined
how this father needs his boy.

# New Normal

I hear of a new normal
of which I want no part.
How can you feel normal
while missing half your heart.

So you can keep the new normal
I prefer the old.
The new is just so empty
hopeless and cold.

Normal is a comfort
that I know I'll never feel.
Disbelief is my companion
no way can this be real.

Aching to return
to the life I once knew.
When I could trust my judgment
on what was real or true.

I can't accept this new reality
nothing seems right.
Can your whole world crumble
in the course of just one night.

*A poetic journey through grief*

So trapped in grief's web
I will forever remain.
I don't even struggle
I welcome all the pain.

It is my only connection
to the one I held so dear.
Embracing the sadness
is an attempt to keep them near.

From this loss, I'll never recover
or be able to move on.
Everything I once lived for
is now dead and gone.

# FAILURE

Fantasy or reality
I can no longer separate the two.
I have lost all distinction
between what is false or true.

I tried to be a good parent
and do what was right.
But my father's role was ended
on that October night.

Suicide had visited
and left a shocking scene.
What kind of father
can't raise a child past fifteen.

All of life's lessons
which I tried to impart.
I must have been a total failure
right from the start.

My boy was happy
at least that's what I thought.
He'll tell me if he's in trouble
well, obviously not.

Every single conviction
which I once held to be true.
Seems in final inspection
I didn't have a clue.

In the reality I once lived
I was my son's best friend.
But how could that ever be
with this tragic end.

# NIGHTMARE

I feel like I've been transported
to a strange and lonely place.
The only familiar sight to me
is that of my own face.

My once warm and happy home
that I loved and knew so well.
Now has been replaced
by a cold and heartless shell.

People here speak of things
to which I can no longer relate.
I keep praying this is a nightmare
so I just sit and wait.

Until the moment I wake up
and my heart will again rejoice.
When I hear the beautiful sound
of your sweet and lovely voice.

I will tell you of my nightmare
and how I love you so.
Then I will wrap my arms around you
and never let you go.

# Return

Return to me for a second
if that's all that you can spare.
Anything to let me know
that you are still there.

A brush on the cheek
or a whisper in the wind.
I will be here waiting
for any message you can send.

Appear in my dreams
so I can hug you so tight.
Sit quietly on my bed
while I sleep at night.

Come hold my hand
when I am missing you so.
Just linger for a minute
and then you can go.

The peace of just knowing
that you are alright.
You could convey
with the presence of your light.

So please come back
and let me know in some way.
Just for a short visit
I know that you can't stay.

Within the gates of Heaven
is where you now reside.
But please return to me often
and stay close by my side.

Until your final visit
when we meet at death's door.
And you'll escort me to Heaven
to part no more.

# VOICE

The loss of my son
has torn my world in two.
Now I have an internal voice
that questions all I do.

Who am I, is a phrase
it will commonly use.
In this never ending battle
I'm destined to lose.

It questions every aspect
of the life I had built.
To make sure I'm drowning
in a constant wave of guilt.

Who am I to get out of bed
and start another day.
Have I already forgotten
about my son, that passed away.

I miss my son so badly
and long to hold him near.
Why am I so tormented
by this voice I'm forced to hear.

I pray for God to quiet it
or grant me a reprieve.
Why must it always question
the way in which I grieve.

*A poetic journey through grief*

I know it must be the devil
determined to destroy.
Every precious memory
ever shared with my boy.


These back and forth discussions
always raging in my mind.
The voice is forever probing
for any weakness it might find.

Losing my son is a nightmare
that was not my choice.
And in his loving absence
I have this sinister voice.

When again in his presence
the questions will finally cease.
And from this bondage
my spirit will get its release

# I Know

When talking to people
about the loss of my son.
They reply to my statements
with "I know" when I'm done.

How could you know
I silently say.
Have you ever suffered
a child passing away.

The hole in your heart
and ache in your soul.
They have to be felt
to imagine the toll.

You would give up your life
for one last embrace.
You are constantly homesick
for the sight of their face.

Just say that you're sorry
and don't try to relate.
It is not possible
unless you share in this fate.

So when you see me hurting
you need not say a word.
Simply give me a hug
and all will be heard.

# HOLE

Who could ever guess
the affliction that I hide.
And all the hurt and pain
going on inside.

For in the center of my heart
there is a gaping hole.
From there it extends
to the depths of my soul.

The love of my son
once filled this vast space.
And only his bright smile
can light up this dark place.

Just beneath the surface
there is a constant dull pain.
That for all my living days
I know will remain.

So I will suffer through this life
and wait for the day.
When the sight of my son
makes this hole go away.

# Pity

I grow so tired of this heartbreak
and can't take it anymore.
I want to return to my old life
the one I knew before.

The role of a victim
just doesn't seem to fit.
I didn't choose this nightmare
but somehow, here I sit.

Each day I try to fool myself
and say I'll be okay.
But the words are so empty
I shouldn't even say.

Just one ray of light
to serve as my guide.
And let me know life is possible
without you by my side.

In all of my dreams
you were a central part.
How can you have a future
when you no longer have a heart.

How do you come to terms
with a reality so bleak.
That to my lovely son
I'll never again speak.

One terrible decision
in a moment of fear.
Has hurt all the people
that held him so dear.

He didn't get the chance
to have a change of heart.
And I'm left to pay the price
with a world torn apart.

# Positive Attitude

My once positive attitude
has vanished in a day.
It left with my son
when he passed away.

In the past I was cheerful
and always wore a smile.
Now each day is painful
every step feels like a mile.

Every piece of my happiness
was embodied in my son.
One month into his absence
the torture's just begun.

From waking in the morning
to going to bed at night.
Each day is like a battle
I lack the will to fight.

My mind deceives my heart
in an attempt to keep me sane.
Trying to convince it,
it can live with all this pain.

How do you pursue a life
when your future is now gone.
I have no other children
I only had the one.

No traditions or memories
to pass down and keep alive.
Only as long as I'm breathing
will they now survive.

*A poetic journey through grief*

The glass that was half full
now lies shattered on the ground.
In the storm clouds overhead
no silver lining can be found.

# Son

Words can never express
all that you meant to me.
You were everything and more
a son should be.

We shared a sense of humor
and at times, it seemed a brain.
Every moment we shared
in my heart will remain.

Your sweet smiling face
is imprinted on my soul.
Only when we are reunited
will I again be whole.

I still talk to you each day
to keep you close and ease the pain.
But until life's journey is over
I know it will remain.

I will honor your memory
in everything I say or do.
And I will be a better person
just because of you.

*A poetic journey through grief*

# GETAWAY

Beach getaway without you
feels so empty and so cold.
Not enough water in the ocean
to drown the sorrows of my soul.

Waves crash into the shoreline
my mind's in another place.
A respite from the here and now
I close my eyes and see your face.

Unable to accept reality
I long to hear your voice.
Dwelling on the day I lost you
a scared reaction, not a choice.

Suicide so full of questions
time can't wash away.
Can you hear me when I call you
please let me know that you're okay.

Sun is shining on the outside
smiling families without a care.
Jealous of their completeness
how can life be so unfair.

No vacation from my heartache
just another place to lay my head.
A change of scenery is pointless
now that part of me is dead.

# One Sound

How can so much destruction
be contained in a single sound.
Leaving my whole world shattered
and crashing to the ground.

The life that I once knew
full of happiness and cheer.
Was destroyed in an instant
by that noise I did hear.

If sound is just a vibration
that travels through the air.
Then how through the very center
of my heart did it tear.

How can so much evil
be contained in a noise.
That will forever isolate you
from all of life's joys.

As quickly as a sound
moves through the air.
My once full life
is now cold and bare.

This beautiful vessel
which I did love and adore.
Now is left forever broken
and lying on the floor.

One shattered silence
so sudden and brief.
Has now left my world
forever incomplete.

*A poetic journey through grief*

Triumph and tragedy
are very close I have found.
They are merely separated
by a solitary sound.

# HE WALKS WITH ME

Although I cannot see him
God walks by my side.
Through the hurt and darkness
He serves as my guide.

The troubles of this world
are one's He understands.
Every tear I've cried
is held within His hands.

On the day I lost my son
He was with me still.
We wept and mourned together
the bitter harvest of freewill.

In the midst of my worlds implosion
God never once left me alone.
At the same time He held my heart
He was walking my son home.

I have to trust in God's wisdom
that He has a purpose for my pain.
Faith is easy in the sunshine
it's only tested in the rain.

When the storms of life are raging
I can take refuge beneath his wings.
And know he won't forsake me
no matter what the future brings.

*A poetic journey through grief*

I continue on in my life's journey
knowing at the end I'll see.
My father who art in heaven
that daily walks with me.

# My Fate

Time may pass without you
but the heartache's with me still.
I dwell on the day I lost you
and fear I always will.

You're enshrined in my heart
as you're weighing on my mind.
The world just keeps on turning
so cruel and so unkind.

They say that it gets easier
I still miss you just the same.
I pray for the peace of heaven
to one day hear you call my name.

This life is now a sentence
which I am forced to serve.
The pain of this existence
no one could deserve.

Left behind to repeat my questions
I guess that's now my fate.
But no answers are forthcoming
but I'll keep asking while I wait.

The inspiration for quite a few of my poems came from the survivors of suicide meetings which I frequently attend. The people that I've met there, now seem almost like an extended family. They were there for me at the darkest point in my life and they offered me encouragement and inspiration through their stories. And for that support and guidance, I will always be grateful. I still vividly remember that first meeting and how I wondered if I was in the right place. Everyone in attendance was smiling and making small talk until 7:30 arrived, then a dark cloud of reality seemed to descend on the room. And as everyone made their introductions and shared about their losses, I could finally see the secret side of suicide loss that remains hidden to most.

## 7:30

Survivors of Suicide meeting
this doesn't look like the place.
The air is filled with small talk
there are smiles on most every face.

But at half past seven
reality descends on the room.
Gone is the illusion of normal
replaced by a real sense of doom.

As the conductor gives his cue
to begin the symphony of pain.
We all shed our outward disguises
that we don in an effort to feign.

Outside we have to appear normal
so we hide behind a false shroud.
We look like a typical person
we try to blend into the crowd.

But in the safety of the circle
the tears can finally flow free.
And you can bare you damaged soul
that few others will ever see.

Temporarily our burdens are lightened
until we pick them back up at the door.
Departing to face the real world
concealing our heartaches once more.

# S.O.S

We sit in a circle
and pour out our souls.
A miserable ring
with hearts full of holes.

Searching for answers
yearning for relief.
From the endless affliction
of perpetual grief.

One by one we speak
and share what's on our mind.
Desperately hoping
some peace we might find.

But comfort will elude us
as we all know.
That only in the next life
will we finally be whole.

## Support Group

I get strength from a group of people
that I wish I had never met.
The reasons we all come together
are ones we would like to forget.

Why can't we still be strangers
out living our lives as before.
Instead of being trapped in this circle
sharing our nightmares once more.

One by one, we state our names
it's like a roll call from hell.
We speak of our loved ones
and the manner in which they fell.

These are the only people
to which I can now relate.
They share in my silent suffering
and know of my tortured fate.

So twice a month you can find me
getting the support to make it through.
All from a group of people
I wish I never knew.

# GATHER

We gather to share the suffering
and tragedy we've known.
Somehow it's a comfort
to know you're not alone.

We share with one another
the hidden burdens that we bear.
Of how we've been cheated
by a life that's so unfair.

Together we empty our hearts
each yearning for relief.
It helps to ease the pressure
but the feeling is brief.

We desperately search for answers
that we know we'll never find.
Questions we keep asking
in our quest for peace of mind.

This secret world of hurt
of which before we never knew.
Now provides the only shelter
from this storm we're going through.

We feel an instant connection
a kinship of the soul.
Joining together in our journey
longing to be made whole

After all is said and done
we know we search in vain.
Until we again see our loved ones
the emptiness will remain.

# THIS WALK

I will walk beside you
down this dark and lonely road.
If you should need someone to talk to
or would like a hand to hold.

I can't offer you any answers
I still have questions of my own.
All I can provide is reassurance
that you don't face this walk alone.

I'm just one of many travelers
on a path I never planned.
Searching for a reason
and trying to understand.

There is safety in our numbers
as we each wage our own war.
To come to terms with our losses
and find a reason to live once more.

We all have different stories
that share in a common end.
The world may desert you
but here you'll always find a friend.

*A poetic journey through grief*

The last two poems that I will share, were written specifically for suicide survivor events. The first poem entitled "Out of the darkness" was read at my local suicide awareness walk which brings hundreds of suicide survivors together, and raises much needed funds and awareness for suicide prevention. The other poem "Survivors Day" was shared at my local International Survivors of Suicide Day event, which takes place worldwide on the Saturday before Thanksgiving. I would strongly encourage you to consider attending events like these in your area, as they really help to fight the feeling of isolation that usually accompanies suicide loss.

# Out of the Darkness

Out of the darkness
step into the light.
No more standing in the shadows,
time to join the fight.

Give a face to suicide,
shed the stigma and the shame.
Rob it of the power
held within its name.

An army of survivors
marching to turn the tide.
In honor of our loved ones,
no longer by our side.

Until this war is over
we'll keep walking every year.
To educate and raise awareness
until we one day persevere

*A poetic journey through grief*

# SURVIVORS DAY

We gather in remembrance
of loved ones we have lost.
We are the aftermath of a suicide
left behind to count the cost.

Tragedy is what unites us
we are wounded, but still alive.
Instead of opting to surrender
we have chosen to survive.

To give a voice to the hidden,
the forgotten and alone.
Survivors who live in secrecy
bearing the burden on their own.

But today we break the silence
and our stories will be told.
Through shared tears and laughter
a sense of purpose will take hold.

We'll leave knowing we can make it
helping each other along the way.
Lost hope will be recovered
on this Survivors Day.

# FINAL THOUGHTS

In closing I would like to leave you with this thought. Although it may be tempting, I hope you resist the urge to rewrite your loved ones entire life story in order to fit their final act. Instead I choose to view suicide as a fatal mistake that was made in the midst of fear, illness or other circumstances. Otherwise suicide has not only claimed our loved ones lives, but also their memories. And those precious memories are all we have to get us through this life. I am truly sorry for your loss to suicide and I sincerely hope that this book has helped you in some small way.

Made in the USA
Lexington, KY
22 January 2019